Pathfinder 23

A CILT series for language teachers

Keeping on target

Bernardette Holmes

Other titles in the PATHFINDER series:

Reading for pleasure in a foreign language (Ann Swarbrick)
Communication re-activated: teaching pupils with learning difficulties
    (Bernardette Holmes)
Yes - but will they behave? Managing the interactive classroom
    (Susan Halliwell)
On target - teaching in the target language (Susan Halliwell and Barry Jones)
Bridging the gap: GCSE to 'A' level (John Thorogood and Lid King)
Making the case for languages (Alan Moys and Richard Townsend)
Languages home and away (Alison Taylor)
Being creative (Barry Jones)
Departmental planning and schemes of work (Clive Hurren)
Progressing through the Attainment Targets (Ian Lane)
Continuous assessment and recording (John Thorogood)
Fair enough? Equal opportunities and modern languages (Vee Harris)
Improve your image: the effective use of the OHP
    (Daniel Tierney and Fay Humphreys)
Not bothered? Motivating reluctant learners in Key Stage 4
    (Jenifer Alison)
Grammar matters (Susan Halliwell)
Differentiation (Anne Convery and Do Coyle)
Drama in the languages classroom (Judith Hamilton and Anne McLeod)
Nightshift - ideas and strategies for homework
    (David Buckland and Mike Short)
Creative use of texts (Bernard Kavanagh and Lynne Upton)
Developing skills for independent reading (Iain Mitchell and Ann Swarbrick)

First published 1994
Copyright © 1994 Centre for Information on Language Teaching and Research
ISBN 1 874016 35 6

Cover by Logos Design & Advertising
Printed in Great Britain by Oakdale Printing Co Ltd

Published by the Centre for Information on Language Teaching and Research,
20 Bedfordbury, Covent Garden, London WC2N 4LB.

Contents

Page

1. **Scenes familiar: recognising the extent of the challenge**   1

2. **Progression: stepping beyond the basic response**   3
   How can we monitor linguistic progression?   5
   So, where are we so far?   8
   The nature of challenge   8

3. **Through the keyhole: a glimpse at successful classroom practice**   12
   Breaking the sound barrier   12
       The Mexican wave
   Using physical response to teach information technology   13
       Partenaires par ordinateur
   Improving memory and accuracy   16
       Dictation with a difference
   Rubrics   16
       Rubric pictionary
   Having your say   17
       Jeu de paraphrase
   The new look vocabulary test   18
   Repair strategies   19
       Y-a qu'à faire un jeu de bof/Na ja Spiel
   Taking the initiative   20
       Résidents du bâtiment B/ Etagenhaus B story
   The extraordinary synergy of independence and creativity   24
       Points en commun/Was haben wir gemein?
   Story-telling and the use of refrains   26
       Objets sous pli cacheté
       Sac à main perdu
   Maximising the use of the survey   29
   Features of activities which help learners keep on target   31

4. 'Second to the right and straight on till morning': a focus on planning 32

Preparing the climate 33

La carte jaune!

Topper/Chapeaux

Avoid random code-switching 34

Being pragmatic about the use of English 34

The query over grammar 35

Consistent approaches from one class to another 35

Breathing life into visuals 37

Displaying language like road signs 37

Responding to learners' needs 37

Use of the grafitti board, notebook or scribble pad 38

5. Reaching for the sky:
questions for self-evaluation and departmental development 39

1. Scenes familiar: recognising the extent of the challenge

Picture the scene - an old demountable at the back of the science block, a damp September, Friday afternoon last period, following a PE lesson and there they all are, our new Year 10 German group, awaiting their first lesson of the new academic year. They have all had opportunities to study German and French in Key Stage 3 but have chosen to continue German up to examination. Some of them come from the same teaching group as last year, but there are many others who come from different groups and one or two who are new to the school. There are also a few from that group that have had three different teachers during the year for various reasons. Unfortunate that! Let us have a look at them!

- **The cognitive analytical learner**
  Well good, there is Rebecca - keen, able, high achieving, participated in the German exchange in Year 9, regular contributor to the class to class mail link with Germany, confident in listening, reading and writing but even after the stay in Aachen, will she use the target language for all classroom communication? Not until she has checked every word in the dictionary and consulted a grammar table, she won't!

- **The communicative interactive learner**
  At least there is good old Darren - always inaccurate, but very willing to have a go. He'll say anything to get his meaning across. To be fair, he is very good at memorising stock phrases, but he doesn't seem to be able to adapt them to new contexts.

- **The divergent introvert**
  Then there is Nassar - very quiet, doesn't seem to be participating in whole class activities, likes to do things his own way, but some of his creative writing is really interesting, even if it wasn't what he was supposed to be doing!

- **The convergent extrovert**
  Whoops! There is Wayne! If you want someone to participate in any class game or quiz, he is the man! Providing he is given clear objectives and sufficient support, he is manageable. Of course, if you are not careful, as he never stops talking, most of his contributions will be in English.

- **The divergent extrovert**
  As for his friend, Kester, well, that is another story. He will not do things your way, and it is not just a question of non-cooperation; he is noisy too and distracts the rest. The only positive influence on him is Wayne.

- **The convergent introvert**
  Thank goodness for Jessica - she may be quiet, but she is so co-operative, presents her work well and is very able to communicate both in speech and writing, if she is not placed in a stressful learning environment.

We have all been there, haven't we? Pre and post the National Curriculum, the challenge of planning progression for such a variety of learners is nothing new. Whatever examination or system of accreditation is adopted for assessment at sixteen, in some senses the teaching and learning programme for 14-16-year olds will always represent a new departure. There may be changes of teacher, changes of group, changes of language. Keeping on target will involve the sensitive combination of recapitulation of what has been done before with the introduction of new areas of content and experience. Expectations of existing knowledge, understanding and skill cannot be taken on trust. What is known will have to be explored and consolidated in such a way that there is always something new and challenging to be experienced in the process.

In terms of pupil use of the target language for the purposes of all classroom communication, every fourteen-year old learner will be at a different stage of development irrespective of ability. Progress in this regard will be affected by previous experience, expectations of both teachers and learners, attitudes to learning and the ethos of the foreign languages department and the school as a whole. All of this, before the significant differences in learning styles are taken into account. Keeping on target for learners in Key Stage 4 presents many challenges for teachers and learners. We will require flexibility in the management of learning and a great variety of approach if we are to meet our target of promoting learner use of the target language.

For those of us following the National Curriculum, where the use of the target language is a statutory requirement, it may be helpful to consider what has been happening so far in terms of pupil response. It would seem that learners are generally responding with enthusiasm to defined content presented and rehearsed in a variety of ways, but are reluctant to step beyond the basic response. They rarely take the initiative or use language spontaneously. Short exchanges in pairs are conducted well, but opportunities to communicate at any length in either speech or writing are more limited.

Before we can help our learners step beyond the basic response, we have to be sure where we are heading. What are the characteristics of the successful language learner? What constitutes progression? How can we build on the foundations of early learning?

2. Progression:
stepping beyond the basic response

- Progression is a feature of effective learning.
- Learning is motivated by our desire to make sense of the world.
- Learning comes through social and cultural interaction.
- We learn through language.
- We need language to make sense of the world.

If these statements are true, there are many implications for progression in language learning.

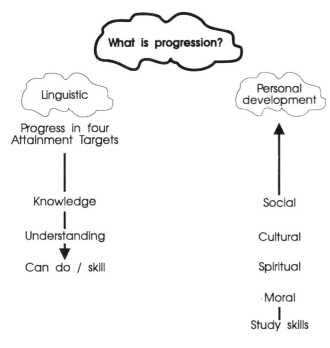

Progression in language learning will hinge on volition, motivation and determination of the learners to communicate in the target language. We will need to provide a range of learning opportunities which, as well as serving to increase the knowledge and understanding of the foreign language, also contribute to personal development. Both the content and the process of learning in the foreign language classroom can be significant in developing aspects of social and cultural development in particular and fostering cross-curricular study skills. We can also make some contribution to spiritual and moral development. No subject of the curriculum is value neutral. Especially in the choice of texts that older learners read, ethical questions of meaning and purpose can be explored. In the following example, the language is straightforward enough to be readily understood, and the content is of significance in making sense of recent historical and political change, as well as offering an opportunity for reflection on the generosity of the human spirit. Why should we not include something like this, when tackling a topic like health and fitness.

> *Histoire de la solidarité*
>
> *Un village en France s'est mobilisé pour soigner un citoyen polonais atteint de cécité, c'est-à-dire aveugle. C'est la preuve concrète, et pour le meilleur, de l'éffacement des frontières Est-Ouest.*
>
> *Darek a onze ans lorsqu'il s'aperçoit qu'il y voit de plus en plus mal. Il doit cesser les jeux qu'il aime tant, le volley, le foot, les médecins consultés lui conseillent de porter des lunettes. Aujourd'hui, trois ans plus tard, Darek a perdu la vision d'un oeil. Il ne distingue ni les formes, ni la couleur, il est atteint d'une tumeur du nerf optique.*
>
> *En Pologne, aucun hôpital ne pratique une telle opération. Alors, les parents tentent l'impossible. Ils partent travailler en Allemagne dans les champs mais la somme récoltée reste insuffisante. Ils pensent alors à la France. Là-bas, près de Lille vit une partie de la famille. Le beau-frère alerté ne se contente pas de contacter le corps médical. Il remue ciel et terre et lance en juillet dernier avec des amis l'association pour Darek et c'est la surprise. En un mois la moitié de la somme a été rassemblée et si les lettres continuent à affluer, l'opération sera envisagée à la fin du mois d'août.*

Learners tend to make greater progress in both spoken and written communication, if they are offered opportunities to invest something of themselves into their learning. Activities must be perceived as relevant. Wherever links in areas of experience exist with other subjects of the curriculum, these should be fully exploited. Links with information technology, personal and social education and the humanities are exemplified in Chapter 3. The desire to communicate must be stimulated. Conceptual bridges should be built between the known and the unknown, while offering opportunities to compare and contrast the self with others. If we expect our learners to communicate, they must have something worthwhile to communicate about.

In terms of the process of language learning ...

- there will need to be a balance between individual, pair and group work;
- whole class teacher-led activities will still be very relevant for older learners but they may need to evolve and take account of learners' ideas to a greater extent;
- equal emphasis should be given to comprehension as well as production - it can be quite demotivating for a learner to find that they are holding a one-way conversation;
- compensation strategies which enable learners to cope with making sense of unfamiliar language when they are not in control should be developed;
- repair strategies such as rephrasing or repeating for clarification can be fostered;
- communication strategies can be encouraged like non-verbal communication and paraphrase;

- a wider range of communication can be expected - transactional exchanges, conversations, presentations and structured talks, discussion and argumentation;
- there can be a greater focus on grammatical awareness and reference skills.

HOW CAN WE MONITOR LINGUISTIC PROGRESSION?

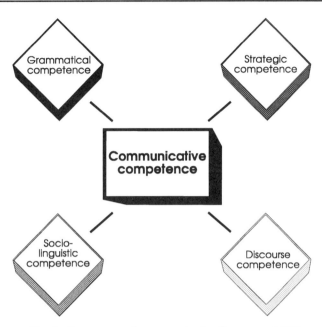

Canale, *Language and commnunication* (Longman, 1983)

It can be helpful to classify progression in terms of grammatical, strategic, socio-linguistic and discourse competence. If we take each of these in turn, we can explore their relevance and value in relation to mapping the progress of our hypothetical learners, Rebecca, Darren, Wayne and co.

Grammatical competence

This is measured by breadth of lexis, awareness of syntax and structure. It can exist and be studied in a decontextualised form (verb tables). Rules can be memorised and tested.

The usage of the term *grammar* can cause some problems:
- do we mean the terminology, e.g. past anterior, preceding direct object?
- do we mean rules, e.g. you make the future tense of regular verbs in *er* and *ir* by taking the infinitive and adding the endings *ai, as, a, ons, ez, ont*?
- do we mean language patterns, e.g. *mit dem Bus, mit dem Auto, mit dem Flugzeug **aber** mit der Straßenbahn*?

5

A performance indicator of grammatical competence is whether Rebecca has sufficient confidence to express an action that took place yesterday, using the perfect tense without checking first in the verb table. Does Darren have enough awareness of grammatical pattern to be able to modify a stock phrase and transfer language to new contexts?

Grammar

Internalising a language system to enable independence.

Richard Johnstone

Strategic competence

This is all to do with linguistic problem-solving, dealing with the unpredictable. What do you do when your existing knowledge of language runs out? Once communication extends beyond defined content, how can you convey a message and stretch your linguistic resources? We are talking about creating metaphors, paraphrase, using communication strategies which combine words and non-verbal communication like mime or gesture, repair strategies like rephrasing or repeating for clarification. Here we are very close to the realm of creativity and imagination.

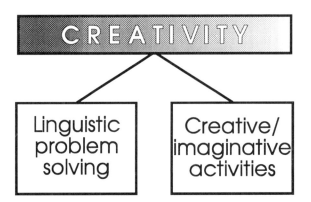

CREATIVITY

Linguistic problem solving

Creative/imaginative activities

Using the language you know to express what you are about to discover.

We can also include under strategic competence the use of reference materials, dictionaries, vocabulary books and simple verbal requests for help and clarification in the target language.

Success in this dimension would see Jessica communicating more readily perhaps, as greater development of strategic competence would certainly reduce the stress in more spontaneous, open-ended speech acts.

Socio-linguistic competence
This is about matching the rules to real purposes appropriately, following conventions of time, place and person. It embraces language functions like greetings, requests, explanations, agreeing and disagreeing, politeness phrases.

Can Wayne use the appropriate register to speak to his teacher or a visitor from abroad?

Discourse competence
This involves more sustained communication, which builds on ideas and may involve a number of different topics. Success is measured by the learners ability to cope with internal structuring, taking the initiative, introducing fresh ideas logically into a conversation or discussion, sequencing ideas coherently and changing topic appropriately. It can be exemplified when learners are required to justify their thinking, hold a multi-person discussion in a group activity, or present information cohesively in a structured talk.

In relation to written communication, there are familiar conventional text types. What tells you that something is a letter, or a play script, a newspaper article, a menu, a poem, a conversation in a novel?

Thinking back to our hypothetical learners, this is an area which is most probably underdeveloped, and yet it is essential if we are to succeed in enabling learners to say what they want to say. There will need to be very specific stages built into activities to allow for the development of discourse competence. This will imply strategic planning over time.

All four dimensions of communicative competence will have an impact on learners' confidence, capability and willingness to use the target language for their own purposes. There is much more to keeping on target than would at first appear.

Independence

Taking control of your use and response to language.

Linguistic management

So where are we so far?

There may seem to be a quantum leap between Key Stage 3 (11-14-year olds) and Key stage 4 (14-16-year olds). In the early years learners are well rehearsed in recognition and response, imitation and production. In order to progress, they are now required to use a range of more complex linguistic and social skills. They may need to negotiate, describe, explain, persuade - all functions of socio-linguistic and discourse competence. It may well be the first time they have been required to do so.

In order to support our learners, we may decide to revisit our teaching approaches and build in opportunities over time for the systematic development of the necessary linguistic skills needed to enable our learners to become more independent users of the foreign language. It could well be profitable to review the range and scope of our teaching programme by evaluating the level and nature of the contribution which particular activities make to overall linguistic progression. How can we help learners to step beyond the basic response?

The nature of challenge

Progression is often a function of challenge. Learning is sometimes described as ineffective, where activities offer insufficient challenge. What exactly does challenge mean in this context? In terms of linguistic demand, it could well relate to the nature and purpose of questioning. We often use quick fire questioning as a device for revising/consolidating items of vocabulary or short single function sentences. This is perfectly appropriate for the specific purpose of acquiring knowledge/vocabulary building. Questions used for this purpose are usually closed - they have only one possible answer. They involve a low level of factual recall and do not place excessive cognitive demands upon the learner. In this respect they do not serve the broader purpose of communication which should embrace choice of response and may involve the expression of thoughts, feelings and opinions. But then, such questioning is not intended to serve this purpose. Perhaps, however, there should be greater emphasis on a balance between closed quick fire questioning and open-ended, probing questioning, which is more thought-provoking. If this is so, there needs to be a necessary shift in the management of class questioning.

Recent work in Australia in primary education reported that teachers ask questions at an average rate of one every twelve seconds. There is a wait time of only one second before a response from the learners is expected! There could be lessons to be learned here in relation to the foreign languages classroom and our quest to develop higher order language outcomes and greater independence. If we ask more demanding questions, we could deliberately leave time for the students to develop their ideas and refine their response. We may wish to build in opportunities to use reference materials or consult with a partner or small group. Providing adequate **wait time** could be a very simple but effective way of moving learners on to produce more thoughtful answers, comments or opinions. In addition, this could create a more reflective environment for the classroom where thinking time and purposeful talk in the target language become part of the culture.

Challenge in relation to the nature of tasks usually relates to the cognitive demands made by the activity. Language is a cognitive process. Activities which rely on low levels of thinking tend to produce low levels of language contribution.

Hierarchy of levels of thinking

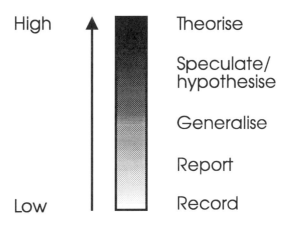

We can increase the level of linguistic and cognitive demand by very simple adjustments to activities. For example, in a matching activity where Christmas presents are linked to a family group whose description is provided, why not remove the family description and ask what kind of a family you think this person may have, if he or she has bought these presents? We are then entering the world of speculation and hypothesis.

Enhanced challenge can also come through the way we organise or contrive the learning situation. The most commonly used model for learning is teacher presentation, whole class practice, followed by further practice in pairs and less often groups. We may find at Key Stage 4 that there may be increased use of the target language by pupils if we are willing to take risks with the model and use more flexible approaches to whole class learning. There can be a healthy balance between activities which have a kick start by teacher stimulus and demonstration and those which begin with the learners' ideas, perhaps through individual to pair to group processes or brainstorming. There can be rich rewards in terms of the quality and range of language used if group work is managed more creatively. Learners can have an individual responsibility to a home group (Figure A). They express their ideas and explore the ideas of others. Opportunities are given to reshape information. The role of the teacher and foreign languages assistant is to support and extend the language used by sensitive intervention. Reference sources must be readily available. The learners then combine in reconfigured groups (Figure B), where they present and share results of their activities. There is further reshaping, collaboration and creative activity. Learners then return to the home groups and present their finished work.

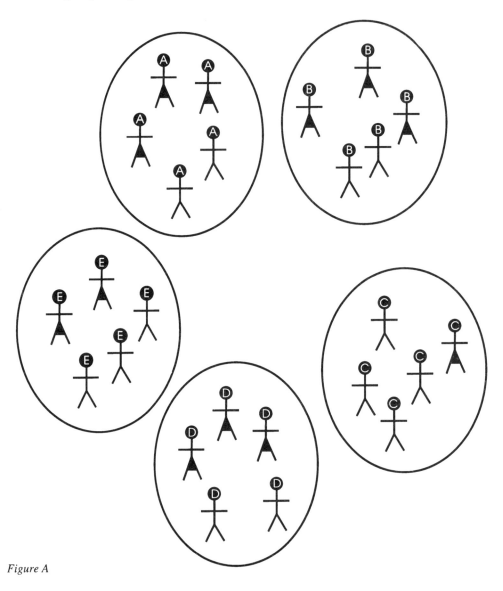

Figure A

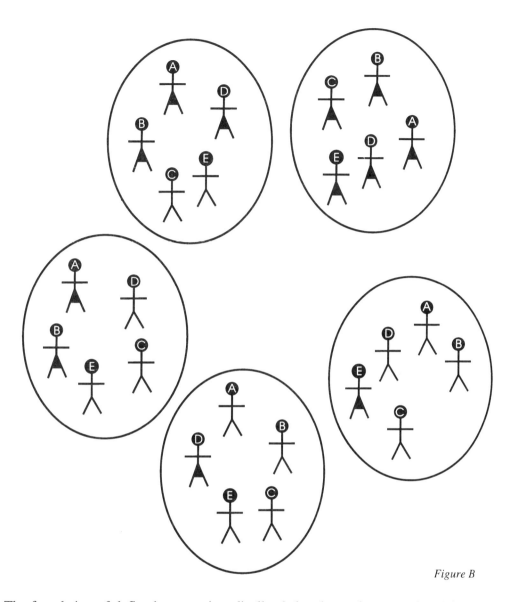

Figure B

The foundation of defined content is radically shaken by such approaches. There may well be a core of language identified by the teacher or course book which is to be included in an activity and explicitly taught. This is highly appropriate, but through the process of creative group work the core will be extended differently according to the language needs of the learners. The agenda for learning is their own. They are saying what they want to say.

3. Through the keyhole: a glimpse at successful classroom practice

Well, straightforward isn't it? In the dynamic learning environment of the foreign languages classroom, immersed as learners are in the target language, how can we fail to produce speakers who are ready and confident to use language for real purposes with increasing competence? If only life were that simple!

If we match the criteria for progression to the characteristics of the successful learner, we are looking at learners who...

- can work independently and co-operatively;
- are confident speakers of the language;
- have aural discrimination acute enough to enable the development of good intonation and pronunciation;
- have a good memory;
- know their way around dictionaries, avid to widen their range of expression;
- have grammatical knowledge sufficient to allow them to adapt previously learned language to new situations;
- can extract meaning and infer mood from spoken and written texts and express their point of view saliently in speech and writing.

All of this, and an increasing sensitivity to and understanding of what being French, German or Spanish really means. Once we start to analyse our expectations, we lay bear the extent of the challenge which they present to teaching and learning. Does this describe many of the learners you teach on a Monday morning? Perhaps it does - perhaps it doesn't. If it doesn't, how can we plan to meet the challenge? What do we need to change in our teaching? What do we need to develop in our learners?

BREAKING THE SOUND BARRIER

Sometimes learners' reluctance to use language more spontaneously is a result of lack of confidence. Perhaps they know and can respond to a range of classroom language but are unwilling to transfer such language to active use because the words are difficult to pronounce. Maybe there was some difficulty in discriminating between the different phonemes making up the word or phrase at the outset, so that the learner is unsure precisely of how you say what you want to say. Some of the words that learners may want to use in the normal business of classroom life, unprompted by the teacher, such as:

Tu as une agrafeuse?   *Passe-moi ton taille-crayon!*

Fais voir ta calculatrice!   *Tu peux distribuer les feuilles?*

may well prove a bit of a mouthful, if they have not been sufficiently well rehearsed at an earlier stage.

We can help learners overcome such problems by making encounters with potentially difficult language more friendly.

- THE MEXICAN WAVE
  Even, and maybe especially, the 14-16-year olds rarely complain at the occasional foray into the world of football mania! Each vertical row or column of the class responds to a separate syllable in a word by raising and lowering their arms, just as in the Mexican wave at the football stadium. Words can be chanted slowly or more rapidly, softly or more loudly and the wave can roll along the rows and back again until the sound barrier is broken and the whole word can be chanted in confidence. The same technique can be used for whole words in sentences to enhance aural discrimination and improve pronunciation and intonation.

Compound words in German can be broken down into their separate parts, for example, *Tages/licht/schreiber.*

Sometimes certain words are more easily rehearsed from the rear, for example, *distribuez - ez... buez... tribuez... distribuez!*

Any innovation is welcome if it achieves the purpose of making language accessible.

USING PHYSICAL RESPONSE TO TEACH INFORMATION TECHNOLOGY

As learners become more mature, the way they learn needs to reflect both the level of their maturity and the complexity of the language and concepts that they are required to understand. There is often a tendency to reduce the amount of physical engagement in the learning the older learners become, because it is felt that active learning is more appropriate for the younger age range. Another way of looking at this could be that the contexts for active learning can become a little more sophisticated along with the learners. Using physical response to teach learners the language and process of creating a database is an example of just such a context.

Création d'une base de données

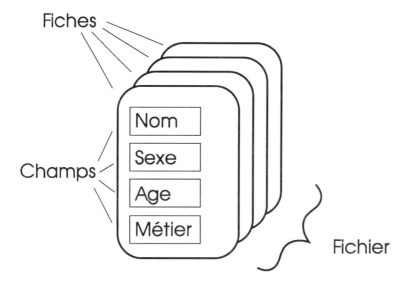

Using a diagram from information technology, which is already familiar to the learners, helps them acquire the new vocabulary. Physical engagement in response to the new vocabulary activates memory. There is also another distinct advantage, physical movement simulating a living database offers a very simple means to understand the process of stacking and sorting information inside the memory of the computer and all that we are doing is asking learners to respond to a range of straightforward questions! So, how is it done?

- PARTENAIRES PAR ORDINATEUR

The class is shown the diagram of the database to present the context and relevant language. If a computer and some software are available in the classroom to serve as real visual aids, so much the better, but it is not strictly necessary for this activity, which is by nature a preparatory activity to using information technology. The class is told that an unspecified person from the lonely hearts column in the newspaper is seeking the perfect partner. The learners are invited to become a living database. In response to a range of questions they move around the room or sit down, simulating the stacking and sorting process of computer memory. The range of questions becomes increasingly more specific, until most of the learners are eliminated. Questioning continues until just one learner fits the bill. At that point the details from the lonely hearts advertisement are revealed. For example:

'M' cherche le partnaire parfait. Voilà, il y a une petite annonce dans le journal. Est-ce que son partenaire parfait est ici parmi vous? On va voir!

On fait semblant. D'accord? La salle de classe s'est transformée en ordinateur. On cherche le partenaire parfait dans une base de données que nous allons créer. Vous, la classe, vous êtes les fiches dans un énorme fichier vivant. Allez-y! C'est parti!

Levez-vous!
Si vous êtes âgés de quatorze à quinze ans, restez debout!
Si vous habitez en Grande Bretagne, restez debout!
Si vous aimez la natation, allez à droite!
Si vous aimez l'informatique, allez à gauche!
Si vous aimez l'informatique et la natation, allez au milieu.
Les autres, asseyez-vous!
Si vous avez un chat, allez à gauche!
Si vous avez un chien, allez à droite!
Les autres, asseyez-vous!
Si vous avez un chat et un chien venez au milieu!
Si vous avez les yeux bleus, allez à gauche!
Si vous avez les cheveux bruns, allez à droite!
Si vous avez les cheveux bruns et les yeux bleus, venez au milieu!
Les autres, asseyez-vous!
Si vous parlez doucement, restez debout!
Tous les garçons, asseyez-vous!
Si vous êtes bavardes, asseyez-vous!
Qui est la plus petite?
Bon, voilà, X, tu es la partenaire parfaite pour 'M', parce que 'M' c'est pour Michel! Bravo!

The stimulus for this kind of activity can vary from a real advert in a French newspaper to something reproduced in the text book, to something invented by the teacher or other learners, maybe from different classes, to the real exchange of particulars with a partner school in France. The ideal follow-up activity is to create a database, using the language and concepts from the demonstration as a stepping stone.

```
Garçon de 15 ans cherche une copine de quatorze
à quinze ans en Grande Bretagne. Passetemps:
l'informatique et la natation. Dois aimer les
animaux - chats et chiens. Petite brune aux yeux
bleus préférée - voix douce, pas trop bavarde!
M
```

Improving memory is important in developing confidence and accuracy in both spoken and written communication. Simple devices borrowed from the English department can assist learners at all stages to improve memory and accuracy, for example **look, cover, write, check**. Most learners can very swiftly copy with accuracy but remarkably few write with accuracy from memory. Activities which focus on memory and accuracy are very useful.

- DICTATION WITH A DIFFERENCE

Dividing the class into two circles, A and B, an inner and an outer, a short text can be photocopied several times and placed on a table or on the floor of the classroom. Learners in the outer circle have to write down the text as dictated by their partners in the inner circle who move swiftly from the text back to their partner, memorising what they have read. There is no restriction on the number of times they can return to the text or on the number of questions in the target language put to them by their partners, but the objective is to produce a fair copy of the text as fast and as accurately as you can. Points are deducted from a hundred for any mistakes made, and the pair with the highest number of points wins. All manner of different texts can be used. Post cards from GCSE papers, simple letters, articles from the newspaper, or just a series of headlines, signs, adverts, whatever is appropriate to the topic of study. The same texts can later be exploited as stimulus material for other activities.

RUBRICS

Rubrics in the foreign language are often the cause of much concern. For the learner whose mustard is not quite so keen as it should be, they provide the perfect excuse for not getting down to work. Authors in the majority of published materials insist quite rightly that all rubrics are given in the foreign language. In most cases, the more frequently used rubrics are also accompanied by some form of simple graphic to assist understanding. Using these graphics in the form of a game can be helpful in familiarising learners with the written instructions that they are likely to encounter in their published course materials. The greater their familiarity with printed instructions, the more confident and capable they become to work more independently.

- RUBRIC PICTIONARY

This is just such a game. All that is required in order to set it up is a scan through the range of published materials or school produced materials in use with the particular class. The rubrics and graphics that learners need to recognise can be gathered together in the form of a list. It is very helpful if they can be photocopied onto a transparency and cut up, so that whole-class warm up activities can be carried out using the overhead projector before the game. As a rule, rubrics should be explicitly taught as and when they occur in the published materials, but like any other language they need to be revisited, otherwise they are all too easily forgotten.

To play the game, learners are divided into three or more teams. The teacher has a set of rubric cards. A member of each team comes up to the teacher and is shown a rubric without a graphic. They have to return to their team and draw or write something to convey the meaning of the rubric. The team has to find the language for the rubric. If they can identify the rubric in English, they gain one point, if they can identify the rubric in the target language they score two points. They can always be encouraged to use their course books for reference material and copy out the appropriate phrases, but this will, of course, slow down the progress of the particular team. On correctly identifying one rubric, another team member will be shown another rubric and so on through the set. The winning team is the team with the highest number of correctly identified rubrics within a given time or on the identification of all the rubrics on the table.

Examples of the kinds of rubrics that are most common and lend themselves to this approach are:

Dessine un cercle.	*Coche ou barre.*
Dessine une flèche.	*Ecris dans le bon ordre.*
Dessine la bonne direction.	*Ecris les lettres.*
Coche la case.	*Ecris le prix.*
Trace la route.	*Coche le bon symbole.*
Remplis la bulle.	*Choisis la bonne réponse.*
Vrai ou faux.	*Remplis la grille.*

HAVING YOUR SAY

When it comes to production of language, expressing themselves in speech and writing, learners need to explore ways of using what they know to convey what they don't know. The mechanisms of paraphrase are invaluable, but if learners are to develop the ability to use paraphrase readily, they must be given opportunities to practise the necessary language and skills and to be sensitive to the different forms of expression appropriate to audience and purpose.

• JEU DE PARAPHRASE

This is an enjoyable and practical activity which requires learners to prepare clues describing a range of familiar objects, without using the appropriate name of the object itself. Instead of the name, a paraphrase is given. For example, a collection of objects, such as a cork screw, a can opener, a paper clip, a drawing pin are gathered together.

The class can be divided into groups. Working together they can devise the clues for each object. The structures which they might employ can be at different levels of complexity:

Un tire-bouchon:
1. *c'est pour ouvrir des bouteilles*
2. *ça sert à ouvrir des bouteilles*
3. *c'est un truc avec lequel on ouvre une bouteille*

Un ouvre-boîte:
1. *c'est pour ouvrir des boîtes*
2. *ça sert à ouvrir des boîtes*
3. *c'est un truc qui ouvre des boîtes*

Une trombone:
1. *c'est pour retenir des feuilles*
2. *ça sert à retenir des feuilles*
3. *c'est un truc qui retient des feuilles*

Une punaise:
1. *c'est pour fixer des feuilles de papier sur le mur*
2. *ça sert à fixer des feuilles de papier sur le mur*
3. *c'est un truc qui fixe des feuilles de papier sur le mur*

Ein Korkenzieher:
1. *damit öffnet man Flaschen*
2. *das braucht man, um Flaschen zu öffnen*
3. *ein Dings, mit dem man Flaschen aufmacht*

Ein Dosenöffner:
1. *damit öffnet man Dosen*
2. *das braucht man, um Dosen zu öffnen*
3. *ein Dings, mit dem man Dosen aufmacht*

Eine Heftklammer:
1. *damit hält man Papier zusammen*
2. *das braucht man, um Papier zusammenzuhalten*
3. *ein Dings, mit dem man Papier zusammenhält*

Eine Heftzwecke:
1. *damit befestigt man Papier an der Wand*
2. *das braucht man, um Papier an der Wand zu befestigen*
3. *ein Dings, mit dem man Papier an der Wand befestigt*

The groups can play a variety of quiz games using the paraphrase clues and winning points by discovering the word for the object described. At a very basic level, *Jeu de paraphrase* can be played by simply using the introductory structure and a non-verbal clue like a mime, e.g. *c'est un truc pour* + an action. However the game is played, dictionaries should be at the ready to extend vocabulary if needed.

THE NEW-LOOK VOCABULARY TEST

It is not always necessary to depart radically from more traditional practice in the quest to keep learners on target. Revamping traditional teaching methods to suit the requirement to use the target language as the normal means of classroom communication can bring rich rewards. The old favourite, the vocabulary test on the learning homework for that week, can have a well deserved lease of life if undertaken in a slightly different way. Instead of showing flashcards or overhead transparencies, and especially instead of using English to test the vocabulary, why not use paraphrase at different levels of complexity? In a mixed ability class, more able learners could be set the task of creating the clues for the class test as an extension of their learning homework.

Average and less able learners could be invited to exemplify specific vocabulary in short sentences:

Benzin   *Ist hier Benzin teuer?*

Benzin ist teuer.   *Nehmen Sie bleifreies Benzin?*

They might be encouraged to keep a recording of what they have learnt on tape. This could be part of their learning homework. Just as they did as younger learners - *une règle, passe-moi une règle, j'ai oublié ma règle* - when they turned their learning homework into something more creative, making a self-help sheet or poster for the classroom wall, or a set of self-help flashcards to be hung up on the washing line across the classroom to encourage more active use of classroom language. For older learners, too, a creative dimension to learning vocabulary is of value.

REPAIR STRATEGIES

A feature which most distinguishes the learner of the foreign language from the native speaker is the inability to flesh out the message or control the pace of an exchange. It is fascinating to listen to people talking on the radio or television, or indeed in the street, and to pick out how many expressions and exclamations are used which are actually redundant to the central message but pad out the communication and allow thinking time, cover up for a hesitation or repair a breakdown in communication. Learners of the foreign language are stranded when they find their own knowledge is deficient or the pace of an exchange is too rapid. They need to make some kind of verbal contribution to show that the lights are on and there is still somebody at home!

• Y-A QU'À FAIRE UN JEU DE BOF/NA JA SPIEL
Keeping a class tally of expressions and exclamations heard in use by the teacher, the assistant, exchange partners or on a tape or video extract is a fun way of extending the range of authentic communication and repair strategies. For example, *J'ai pas*; *Je ne sais pas moi*; *Si tu veux*; *Comment dirais-je?*; *Enfin*; *Bref*; *Allez*; *Non*; *Mais c'est pas ça, quoi!*; *BOF!*; *Vielleicht*; *Sicher*; *Weiß nicht!*; *Meinetwegen!*; *Na ja, kann sein!*; *Wirklich?*; *Mal sehen...* etc. A good game can be to put some of these expressions on card. Learners draw one at random and are invited to build it into their GCSE role play to add a touch of authenticity. Gradually, familiarity with the kinds of expressions used begins to permeate the learners' language and they start to use the expressions as the

need arises naturally. Introducing the occasional idiomatic phrase or structure and setting a challenge to the learners to use the phrase whenever appropriate is another way of stimulating language use, for instance, how many times can you use the construction *Y-a qu'à + l'infinitif*, e.g *Y-a qu'à changer d'activité!*; *Y-a qu'à regarder dans le dictionnaire*; *Y-a qu'à faire un jeu maintenant*, etc.

TAKING THE INITIATIVE

Encouraging learners to take the initiative is something to foster early on in the learning. Techniques which build on learners' ideas and enable them to transfer what they know to fresh contexts go a long way to promoting a more dynamic learning environment. Learners are more willing to take risks and volunteer contributions where they feel that their ideas are valued and are a central part of the learning process. A culture of creativity is developed.

Techniques such as **slow-reveal**, where learners volunteer ideas in relation to the identity of a visual that is slowly revealed to them, and **prediction**, where something is hidden and learners suggest as many ideas as they can until the correct idea is given, are an essential starting point in developing independence and creativity. As the body of known language expands, we can exploit techniques such as brainstorming **'un remue-méninges'** more fully.

- RÉSIDENTS DU BÂTIMENT B/ETAGENHAUS B STORY

This activity begins with a demonstration involving the whole class of how to create a character from a picture. Using one of the pictures on an overhead transparency, the slow-reveal technique is used, covering the whole picture with a piece of card and gradually drawing back the card to reveal more and more detail progressively in response to ideas elicited from the learners.

A whole range of questions can be used from the very simple to the more complex, to prompt suggestions and ideas from the class.

Qu'est-ce qu'il y a sous la carte? Un animal, un fruit, un légume, une personne? C'est quoi, à votre avis?
Was haben wir hier? Was für ein Bild ist das? Ein Tier, Obst, Gemüse, eine Person, oder? Keine Idee! Haben wir Vorschläge?

The card is slowly drawn down to reveal the top of the head.

Une personne? D'accord!
Genau, eine Person!

Further detail is slowly uncovered.

Un homme ou une femme? Un garçon ou une fille? Bon, oui, c'est ça, c'est une femme.
Mann oder Frau? Junge oder Mädchen? Gut, richtig. Wir haben hier eine Frau.

In the early stages of the activity the necessary language and concepts to answer the questions can be supplied, so that all the learners are required to do is to observe and select the appropriate response. As the activity progresses, a greater degree of choice is offered and greater scope for individual opinion is provided.

Contente ou mécontente?
Froh oder traurig?
Elle est comment, cette femme? Belle ou moche? Pourquoi?
Wie sieht sie aus? Schön oder häßlich? Warum?

Justification for the answers must always be sought. The visual is nearly entirely revealed.

Elle est de quelle âge? Vous avez une idée?
Wie alt ist sie? Eurer Meinung nach?

The visual is gradually completely revealed, as the class suggests possible ages.

Vingt ans, trente ans. Cinquante ans, vous dîtes!
Zwanzig. Dreißig. Fünfzig Jahre alt, habt ihr gesagt?

The whole picture is now projected. The brainstorming process has been well established by the slow-reveal technique and can be pursued further. More complex and sophisticated questions can be introduced, which make greater linguistic and cognitive demands on the learners.

Eh bien, vous avez dit cinquante ans. Pourquoi?
Warum habt ihr fünfzig Jahre alt gesagt?

Teacher gives adequate time for reflection and the formulation of appropriate reasons.

Ah! Par sa façon de s'habiller. Oui. Parce qu'elle est grosse. Elle a l'air fatiguée. Oui, elle a le front ridé. Elle porte des bottillons montants (slipper boots)! C'est possible, oui. Dans la rue! Vous croyez?

In the true spirit of brainstorming, all ideas, however unusual, are listened to and given respect. Certain ideas are then built on to prompt further contributions and create the need for more language.

D'accord. C'est intéressant! Si, je vous propose, qu'elle a trente ans. Qu'est-ce que vous diriez?

Interessant, na! Wie wäre es mit dreißig Jahren alt?

A range of opinion can be gathered from the class. Other questions can be posed in relation to the possible jobs that the characters may undertake, what kind of family they might have, their nationality, their character. Once the class is accustomed to this style of learning, opportunities can be taken to explore stereotypes and challenge some of the more entrenched ideas expressed and a full class structure can be built according to learners' agenda, enabling them to say what they want to say.

Time must always be allowed for learners to refine what they want to say, have recourse to reference materials like their vocabulary books, glossaries, bi-lingual dictionaries or in the case of 'slipper boots', the mail order catalogue! If English is used to express an opinion which the teacher or assistant then translates into the required foreign language, opportunities for recapitulation by the learners of some of the previous ideas using the target language need to be ensured. As ideas are gathered from the learners, they can be noted down on the whiteboard for all to share.

In the next lesson the learners are divided into groups of six. Each group has a different character to invent, so that Group A could be creating a character for a little boy in a striped T-shirt, Group B could be inventing a character for a severe looking man with a sneer and a bald head and so on. Each member of the group is given a copy of the same character to look at, so that the first stage of the activity can be conducted individually.

Individual work
The learners are invited to engage in the same sort of process that has previously taken place at whole class level. They firstly have to look at their own picture and note down their ideas in rough about the person. They are recording and describing what they see. They can then enter the realm of creativity and imagination. Who is this person really? How do they feel? Why? Do they work? If so, what do they work at? And what about their family and friends, pets and so on?

Pair work
Once individuals have noted down their initial thoughts, these are then shared with a partner. At this stage similarities and contrasts can be identified and ideas can be refined. In mixed-ability situations a great deal of support and extension can take place by sharing ideas between partners of different ability.

Pair to group work
The separate pairs then join together as a full group and present their ideas. Ideas can be judged as good or bad and retained or rejected until the group agrees their best version of a character. If there are equally strong and feasible versions that is fine, they can all be respected and used for the next stage of the activity.

Individual reflection
After time for group discussion, each individual learner must have adequate opportunity to draft and redraft a written description of the agreed character, or an individual version, if preferred. It is at this point that greater focus must be given to accuracy.

Reconfiguration of groups
Using the model referred to in Chapter 2 (pp10-11), the home groups are reconfigured, so that each new group comprises one member from each of the original groups. We now have a situation where each individual learner has taken charge of the personality that they have created and has joined with a fresh group of learners, each in possession

of a different character card. The class is then told that all of these characters live in the same block of flats, *Résidents du bâtiment B/Etagenhaus B*. They are set the task of deciding what relationships if any exist between the characters and to invent the introductory episode of a soap opera about them.

The process of brainstorming ideas, where each learner makes a contribution and every contribution is noted down for consideration at a later stage is the best way of proceeding. Ideas are refined. Storylines are agreed. Reference sources are in very active use until a version is completed. Once again time must be built in for a written version to be drafted and redrafted with a focus on accuracy.

Peer group evaluation
The learners with their completed versions return to the home groups. There are now six versions of the soap opera. Each individual learner can present their version to the home group. This can involve just reading their written account or they can use the pictures as prompts and try to tell the story from memory. The group decides which version is the most exciting and why. The results of each group's deliberations are shared with the whole class and the version which has the most votes is presented to the whole class. It can later be turned into a play script and put on video, if resources allow. A selection of the soap operas can be mounted and displayed for other learners in other classes to read and enjoy.

THE EXTRAORDINARY SYNERGY OF INDEPENDENCE AND CREATIVITY

It can be seen that the kinds of teaching approaches most effective in developing learner independence have much in common with those which promote creativity. To succeed in developing independent use of language, we first have to stimulate the desire to communicate. Activities should entice learners to take the initiative. To progress, learners have to extend the boundaries of their knowledge and skill to the limit, generating the need for more language. To develop confidence in the use of communication strategies, they have to be put in situations where they edge forward from what is known to what is unknown, rather than be forced to make a perilous quantum leap. Here are some examples of further activities which open the door to learner independence and creativity.

- ### POINTS EN COMMUN/WAS HABEN WIR GEMEIN?
A straightforward survey on a range of current topics can be extended to include opportunities to rehearse communication strategies and be inventive with known language to convey or understand new language. Learners can be invited to interview each other on three or four prepared topics and to gather information on a interview grid.

Name	Familie	Haustiere	Schulfächer	Hobbies	Geheimnis

Topics could be the usual things like family, pets, schools subjects, hobbies. There is then the magic ingredient. Learners are asked to fill in something secret about themselves, something funny or special, which although secret, they don't mind sharing. All manner of secrets pour forth. The language is new and learners need support from the teacher, the foreign language assistant or the dictionary to complete their special square. The survey is then taken around the class with learners filling in the details of their friends. In the given range of topics, most learners are rehearsing and consolidating known language, when it comes to the secret square, they are obliged to ask for clarification, use compensation and communication strategies and on occasion refer to the dictionary. At the end of the activity, they can find out what they have in common and report back or write up a profile on one or more of their friends.

The secrets discovered can be written up onto a quiz sheet or individual cards. These can then be used as a guessing game - whose secret is this? In groups, learners can hold a brief discussion **in the target language** as to whose secret they have. The class then comes together to hear the verdict. In all such activities, it is insufficient to read the secret and then just say a name. Spokespersons for each group have to justify their choice. The cardinal rule is always follow the process of *Qui est-ce? Pourquoi? Parce que .../Wer? Warum? Weil... .

'New' language encountered through the process of the activities can be noted down in a rough book or at the back of a vocabulary book as they go along. At this stage inaccuracies are inevitable and are an implicit part of the learning process. When it comes to writing up or presenting the information, learners will have the appropriate opportunity to refine what they have noted down. They will be encouraged to use dictionaries, grammatical tables, glossaries, as well as refer to their teacher or their peers using the target language. Where Information Technology is in use to present a written profile, perhaps in the form of a magazine page or class newspaper, drafting and redrafting opportunities can be exploited fully.

Not all activities can result in a product, as such. Sometimes the process is sufficient in itself. However, generally, there is still a considerable amount of writing going on in our classrooms in Key Stage 4 and it is always a good idea, wherever possible to give writing an up-market focus by producing something of high quality which can be retained and displayed. If learners' writing can also be used as a stimulus for reading and discussion for other learners, that is always a bonus.

This activity takes its inspiration from the delightful children's story *The hungry caterpillar* by Eric Carle. By awakening childhood memories of the simple discourse pattern used in the story, grammatical awareness can be raised of the use of the perfect and imperfect tenses. Using the stimulus of a version in French, *La vie de Mange-tout la chenille... Lundi elle a mangé un citron, mais elle avait toujours faim! Mardi, elle a mangé deux bananes, mas elle avait toujours faim! etc,* substituting an increasing number of different fruits for each day of the week, the use of the perfect tense and the use of the imperfect in the refrain can be consolidated as a whole class oral activity. Once the pattern is identified, it can be adapted to other characters invented by the teacher or the learners themselves, for example:

Archibavard

qui a passé une
heure au téléphone,
mais qui ne voulait
toujours pas raccrocher

Supersportif

qui a pris une heure
d'exercice avant le
petit déjeuner,
mais qui ne voulait
toujours pas s'asseoir!

SUPERPOUBELLE
Superpoubelle - Lundi, elle a recyclé un vieux frigo, mais elle voulait toujours recycler autre chose!

The application of the grammatical pattern to more whimsical and sophisticated contexts makes a closer match to the interest of the learners and avoids insulting their maturity. There is a link in terms of the content of some of the stories to other areas of the curriculum, health and fitness, protection of the environment. In the case of *Superpoubelle*, not only is the story and refrain relevant and stimulating but she can also inspire a song!

To be sung to the tune of Abba's *Super trooper*:

Superpoubelle, protégez la terre!
Plastique! Ordures! Verre!
Vous recyclez tout!
Notre avenir, c'est vous!

Setting up the story-telling activity in the classroom follows a very similar process to that described previously in the *Residents du bâtiment B/Etagenhaus B* story. To begin with, there is a whole class demonstration of the pattern and story-telling procedure. Groups of learners are in charge of a day each of the *Mange-tout* story, while the whole class chants the refrain. The class is then divided into groups, with each group inventing a similar story type and refrain for a variety of characters supplied by the teacher. Each group is in charge of creating one story. The groups are reconfigured, so that each learner can take their story and set it up actively with a new audience. They then take it in turns to be narrator of the main part of the story in the perfect tense with the rest of the group chanting the refrain in the imperfect tense.

The next activity involves the learners remaining in their reconfigured groups and creating characters of their own device. These are then taken back and presented to the home groups. The home groups select the best characters in their opinion and these are performed by the class as a whole. Every learner is offered the opportunity to present and illustrate their own character. These can be published in a class story book for other learners to read.

- OBJETS SOUS PLI CACHETÉ

The principle of hypothesis and justification is behind this activity, which is designed to provide a context for preparing the topic lost property. The individual contents of a handbag are put into numbered brown envelopes and sealed. The class is divided into groups. Envelopes are passed from group to group. Learners can feel, shake, weigh and smell the envelopes but, of course, they must not open them. They discuss in the target language and decide on the nature of the object(s) within the envelope. They make a suggestion and give reasons for their choice. Dictionaries are available to help them.

The activity is not purely valuable for the language it stimulates, but also for the social and discursive skills required: expressing an opinion, disagreeing, making alternative suggestions and so on. Before the learners begin the activity, it can be helpful to demonstrate very briefly in front of the class how to go about the process and engage in the discussion. This can involve just the teacher verbalising what they are doing and thinking, using expressions like, *A mon avis, je crois, je ne suis pas sûr(e), ça sent bon/mauvais, c'est grand/petit, léger/lourd, long/court, en plastique, en bois*, etc, or preferably involving both the teacher and the assistant or perhaps a sixth form student of language, so that a discussion and exchange of views can be demonstrated - *non, ce n'est pas ça, je crois, je ne suis pas d'accord*, etc. The activity can be made as structured or as unstructured as necessary to suit the aptitudes of the learners. It can be supported by a self-help sheet or transparency of expressions and specific vocabulary to describe particular objects, or it can be completely open-ended. If a self-help sheet is to be used, it should never be too long or it ceases to be of value! A good compromise is to give a start on the self-help sheet, perhaps divided into three categories, some expressions of agreement, some expressions of disagreement, some adjectives with space for the learners to fill in anything else that they learn in the process of conducting the activity.

- SAC À MAIN PERDU

This activity lends itself to a variety of different levels of task. Handbags are used again, one per group. They contain all sorts of different objects and printed material, such as keys, wallets, spectacles and so on, cheque books, tickets, appointment cards, shopping lists, receipts, letters, birthday cards, telephone messages, anything that can be acquired from colleagues or the foreign languages assistants and is authentic and 'real'. It is allowed to contrive some contents to suit your purposes and serve the interests of creativity! It will involve learners in reading and writing, speaking and listening. The first written task is straightforward, just making an inventory of the contents. The contents of the bag can be unpacked and shared around the group. From known language they can note down items that they can already identify in the foreign language. Then asking each other or their teacher, or by using reference materials, they can discover the language for the rest of the contents. The group must come to an agreement, through discussion in the target language, as to whose bag it could be. There are no right or wrong answers.

Depending on the amount of written material included, the activity can be organised at various levels of complexity, using various time frames. Who are they? What were they doing when they lost the bag? What did they buy at the supermarket? Where did they visit recently? Where will they be going soon? A range of factual information can be sought and reported back. Then we can move on to more demanding and higher order skills. Taking a look at the shopping list, what does this tell you about their likes and dislikes, social life, family life? Looking at the cheque book stubs, what do they spend their money on? What kind of person are they? From reading a letter or short note, what further information can be discovered about the lifestyle and character of the person?

MAXIMISING THE USE OF THE SURVEY

In early language learning surveys are used frequently as a means to practise simple questions and answers. For older learners the survey can fully come into its own and serve a much wider purpose. Using the home group model once again (pp10-11), learners can prepare questions on different topics, *Freizeit und Hobbies*, *Transportmittel, Eltern, Schule, Umweltschutz, Einkaufen, Feiertage und Ferien usw.* The questions can be devised firstly individually, then shared with a partner and where necessary refined. Then working as a whole group, all the questions are pooled and classified into a working survey. If resources allow for the use of information technology, the preparation of the interview grids can be undertaken by the learners to add a touch of class and professionalism to the survey activity. A variety of subjects can be chosen for interview. Learners can interview other groups within the class and conduct a survey of the peer group, or of another class within the school, or send their surveys to the partner school abroad, or interview the exchange students. The examples given are of interest as they were designed by learners in mixed age groups ranging from twelve to seventeen years of age. They were then used in the high streets of France and Germany as part of a Young Reporter study visit. Recordings of the interviews were made on cassette and learners used the tapes to make transcripts of their conversations on their return home.

29

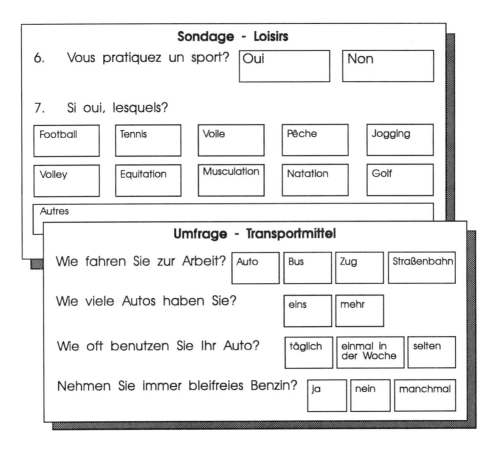

Whomever the survey samples, whether the peer group or native speakers, what happens to the findings is crucial. A great deal of investment of time and energy has gone into the preparation of the interview grids and corresponding questions, and it is therefore more valid as an activity if an equal investment of time and energy is expended in the follow-up activities. Each individual learner has a unique responsibility to the home group. They are team players as well as individual learners. In the process of the survey they are charged with noting down the information, keeping an accurate record of what has been said and by whom. Once back to the home group, the findings can be shared and analysed. There is then opportunity for generalisations to be made on the findings and reported to the class as a whole. It may be appropriate for the group to choose a spokesperson to report back to the whole class on behalf of the group, but this can sometimes be stressful for the learners and less productive for the rest of the class than we would wish. Using the strategy of reconfigured groups, every learner can be involved actively! As each home group will have prepared a report on a separate topic, in the reconfigured groups each learner can present their individual report as a structured talk from notes. The noise levels should be quite acceptable as at any one time only one learner from each group should be reporting back. Questions for clarification or repetition from other learners should always be in the target language. A final written report on all of the different topics can be compiled and circulated to every learner.

FEATURES OF ACTIVITIES WHICH HELP LEARNERS KEEP ON TARGET

The kinds of process used in these activities develop creativity and independence. As well as on linguistic benefits, emphasis is placed on mutual respect for the ideas and contributions of others. Within the different stages of the activities, there is a shifting emphasis from encouraging the expression of ideas, which stretch linguistic resources and possibly may result in a degree of error along the way, to the focus on the refinement of form and attention to accuracy. Early intervention by the teacher to correct innaccuracies may result in curbing learners' initiative and readiness to say what they want to say. As they refine the content of their contributions for specific purposes, they also improve the quality of their communication and seek to express themselves as coherently and accurately as possible. They invite intervention. It is the learners who are setting the pace and the direction of the activities and the approach to grammar and accuracy is more 'learner driven' (Hawkins E, 'Percept before precept', in King L and P Boaks, *Grammar! A conference report* (CILT, 1994)).

These activities are just examples. They may or may not appeal to all teachers or indeed to all learners, but what is interesting about them is that they all have certain features in common:

- they combine two or more of the four language skills;
- they allow learners to move from what is known to what is unknown, dealing gradually with more complex language and tasks;
- they stimulate interest in using reference sources;
- they offer opportunities to use compensation strategies and communication strategies, developing learners' potential to solve linguistic problems and deal with the unpredictable;
- they develop discursive skills, for example, expressing agreement and disagreement, making suggestions, taking turns, etc;
- they offer a range of different writing opportunities, from noting down information from spoken input, noting down discoveries from reference sources, collecting ideas from discussion, to drafting and redrafting creative writing, to making a written presentation or delivering a structured talk from notes;
- they foster a healthy attitude towards error, which can be seen as a stepping stone towards greater accuracy appropriate to audience and purpose in both spoken and written presentation;
- they widen the learners' range of structure and vocabulary according to the learners' agenda as well as the teachers';
- they offer learners the chance to explore the culture of the countries where the target language is spoken. Progress is made in all four language skills through the promotion of active involvement and the development of oracy. Our learners are beginning to step beyond the basic response.

4. 'Second to the right and straight on till morning': a focus on planning

When Peter told Wendy the way to his address in the Neverland,
'second to the right and straight on till morning',
he was just saying the first thing that came to his head.
(J M Barrie)

Classrooms where learners are ready to use and respond to the target language as the principal source of communication should not be a Neverland. They can and do exist. Getting there is not easy. Enabling learners to say what they want to say, as well as to say what we want them to say, requires very careful and systematic planning. Saying the first thing that comes into our heads or, indeed, verbalising everything indiscriminately will not in itself enable learners to become independent users of the language themselves. In terms of classroom language and the management of learning, we need to be selective and focused about what we say and how we say it. The simpler we can be the better. We have to make decisions about what is essential for learners to use and understand and what is less important. When it comes to planning content, we have to make room for the learners' ideas.

As we continue to develop our policy and practice for 14 to 16-year olds it can be helpful to take account of their early experience of learning through the target language and consider their views.

> **It might have been easier if I'd known what to expect!**

Learning takes place through voluntary interaction. In the foreign languages classroom there is a delicate balance between the teacher presenting language and the volition of the learners to accept and respond to that language, making it their own. Even in departments where approaches to using the target language are shared, learners can feel excluded by a code of practice that only teachers have designed and agreed. Learners may feel threatened by immersion in what could be perceived as an alien whirlpool of sound.

Much of the threat can be alleviated if learners are psychologically and emotionally prepared before they enter the foreign languages classroom. They will feel comfortable if what they experience meets their expectations. If they understand how the classroom operates, they will be more willing to participate in language learning activities. They need to know where to turn to for support. The earlier they can begin to take some responsibility for their own progress, the better. The earlier they experience success, the more motivated they will be to pursue their learning and persist in ever more challenging language situations.

PREPARING THE CLIMATE

Even with older learners, embarking on examination courses, it isn't too late to conduct an initial discussion in English about what to expect, inviting learners to ask questions and express their feelings about taking their language learning further. Learners often have a wealth of ideas of how to improve the learning situation. They can suggest ways in which their teachers can help them overcome reluctance towards learning through the target language. They can put forward their own additional ideas about classroom management, support materials, what could go on to wall displays, which is relevant for the older learner. They enjoy thinking up strategies to encourage each other to increase the length of time that they are willing to sustain the use of the target language, conventions for bailing out and so on. Here are two examples of strategies devised by learners.

- ## LA CARTE JAUNE!

In some ways, learning through the target language is a game and pupil use of the target language is the principal rule. Given the opportunity, learners are often very willing to join in as referees, controlling those players who break the rules of the game by too readily reverting to the use of English. A player who persists in using English, despite a warning, is shown the yellow card. Three offenses and it is the red card; the player is 'booked' and is given a punishment by the referee and the other players (the rest of the class). This could range from singing *Frère Jacques* solo to reciting a French verb to copying out a chunk of the glossary from the text book. Whatever it is, the discipline is in the hands of the referee for that day - one of the learners!

- ## TOPPER/CHAPEAUX

Particularly in the East End of London, there is a popular phrase, *Topper*, which is used whenever one person can outdo the other. A French version of this could be *Chapeaux*. A selection of phrases commonly used in the classroom can be put onto cards. With a partner, learners can have a go at drawing out a card from the pack *Pioche*. They then have to use the phrase appropriately as often as they can in a given lesson or series of lessons. Every time they use the phrase they score a point. The partner who uses the phrase the most frequently is the winner, *Topper/Chapeaux*. The strength of this activity is that the learners are motivated to use the language without the intervention of the teacher alongside other activities and are also their own arbiters as to whether the language has been used in an appropriate context. As learners are always keen to get their own back, they usually return eagerly for another card, so that *Topper/Chapeaux* can become an on-going strategy which expressly promotes increased use of the target language.

The fact that learners have taken part in the discussion and perhaps agreed certain strategies with their teachers creates a co-operative environment in which some of the immediate needs of both teachers and learners have been identified and addressed. It is never too late for a fresh start.

> **Sometimes, I don't know whether it's French or English in my lesson.**
> (a non-native speaker of English)

Random code-switching from one language to the next and back again is likely to prove detrimental and confusing for most learners, not least of all those for whom English is not their mother tongue. Where there is uneven use of the target language for whatever reason, we can build in teaching strategies that prevent frequent and random code-switching from English to the foreign language. The example of the learner who could not tell whether French or English was being spoken in the lesson is a salutary one.

AVOID RANDOM CODE-SWITCHING

It is important to make it quite clear when we intend to use the foreign language exclusively and when it is appropriate to revert to English. There are parallels with drama, stepping in and out of role. In fact, techniques borrowed from drama can be very effective. Clear signals can be adopted by all members of the department, such as clicking your fingers to indicate that everyone is now expected to use the target language until a further signal is given. We could encourage a little cultural awareness in French classes by using a theatrical convention, *les trois coups*, instead of striking three blows on the stage with a mace, three single beats of a fist on the table are enough to show that the curtain is rising and our classroom performance, or indeed, rehearsal, is expected to be in French. Visuals can also be of assistance. Flags can be used for a number of purposes - by the teachers to indicate stepping into or out of using a particular language, by learners requesting clarification in a particular language or permission to use a particular language, e.g. *Auf Deutsch, bitte! Darf ich Englisch sprechen? C'est quoi en français?* pointing at the relevant flags on the wall.

BEING PRAGMATIC ABOUT THE USE OF ENGLISH

If we feel that English has a place at some point in a lesson or series of lessons, then it is probably more beneficial to be systematic about including it in our lesson plans from the outset, rather than slip into English by default. It may be that we require learners to reflect on the foreign language they have been using, and make comparisons with the knowledge of the mother tongue. This could be to promote grammatical and socio-linguistic skills, where explicit reference to the mother tongue may accelerate understanding as a prelude to more extensive study of the target language.

THE QUERY OVER GRAMMAR

In developing grammatical awareness, there may be times when it is perfectly appropriate to study the rules and forms of language in a decontextualised manner. We might for example take a familiar text and invite learners to extract all the adjectives or verbs denoting actions that happened in the past and ask them to investigate the words, recognise patterns and deduce rules. It is part of the cognitive process of learning a second language that comparisons and parallels will be drawn from knowledge and experience of the mother tongue. It may be that some of the grammatical analysis is quite properly undertaken for a short time in English in the interests of developing effective language awareness. However, in a classroom where the culture of using the foreign language has become second nature, learners will gradually feel ready to discuss their discoveries using the target language. There may be times when two-language conversations work to good effect, where the learner is using English but the teacher responds in the target language. We can afford to be pragmatic. The kind of decontextualised analytical activity described above can occupy a valuable place in language learning, providing that there are swift follow-up opportunities to match linguistic discoveries to real purposes and set language forms into living functional communication.

I don't know how to tell my partner what to do.

CONSISTENT APPROACHES FROM ONE CLASS TO ANOTHER

Within the classroom, where the explicit aim is for pupils to use the target language themselves for real purposes, strategies which encourage pupils to share in the control and management of learning bring a number of instant advantages. The language of classroom routines, instructions, demonstrations, evaluation, praise and discipline will have been in regular use from class to class. If we have been consistent, particularly in the early years, in the choice of language we use, rehearse a dictionary of gesture between colleagues, create and share a bank of visuals to support meaning, learners will gain confidence in using and responding to the target language in a variety of situations. The divisions of responsibility for the day to day business of the classroom between teacher and learner can become progressively more blurred. Learners can be invited to assume the role of the teacher, giving instructions, demonstrations, explanations to the whole class. They can organise their own resources, choose their own partners or groups, discuss and evaluate their work, using a defined range of language from a very early stage.

Language needs will vary from one activity to the next. For older learners, the complexity of higher order language activities will require a greater range of language to explain the process. If learners are to be involved in using the target language, both as the medium as well as the object of study, careful analysis of the language required to set up and conduct activities should be taking place regularly from lesson to lesson. As we plan our lessons and scheme of work, it may be valuable to think of such language as a discrete area of content, entitled perhaps 'task-specific language'. Learners should be reminded that language use is the means to an end as well as the end itself. Task-specific language will be of equal importance as any other area of content, but it should be as simple and unambiguous as possible.

Defining appropriate phrases for the learners to use in the form of lists can serve as a useful aid to planning and helpful reference for non-specialist staff. However, generally it is only in the context of the classroom supported by gesture, mime and a visual prompt, if possible, that the agreed body of language comes to life. If learners are to fully understand, recall and use language pertinent to the process of learning, such language should be explicitly addressed in as many exciting ways as other aspects of language content. Language needs can be negotiated in discussion with the learners themselves.

The funny little pictures on the wall used to help, didn't they?

Yeah! But I know those ones. I need new ones to say what I want to say.

Learners can develop increased independence through interaction with their environment. The use of posters and mobiles displaying key elements of classroom language can be very helpful for younger learners in promoting understanding and response to instructions, explanations, rubrics and so on. This is especially so when consistent visual support has been given, so that the symbol associated with the instruction is the same, or sufficiently similar, on the wall as it is on the worksheet or text book. What does the older learner need? Are there any damage limitation strategies which could increase the amount of target language in use by more reluctant learners at KS4?

BREATHING LIFE INTO VISUALS

Displaying language supported by visuals can promote understanding and response, but in itself cannot ensure transfer into active use. Learners' confidence and response are best when the language is explicitly and regularly taught in a variety of active ways, such as team games and quizzes, for example 'Give us a clue' using the language of classroom instructions and requests. Visual prompts can be reproduced on flashcards or mini-flashcards and used in pair work or card games. These offer plentiful opportunities to rehearse the language of classroom management and everyday needs and in so doing should also provide 'real life' contexts in which to apply the same elements of language. Self-help material can be produced, using the same visuals for learners to keep with them wherever they happen to be taught in the school, even if it is in the old demountable at the back of the science block.

DISPLAYING LANGUAGE LIKE ROAD SIGNS

Arrête

Travaille avec moi

Puis-je travailler avec l'assistante?

Kann ich helfen?

Ich verstehe!

Ich bin an der Reihe

37

Appropriate self-help visuals can be displayed which are relevant to the nature of that particular activity. Self-help visuals need to be context-related. Displays need to be frequently changed. Alternative means of displaying visual support can be developed further, such as building up a bank of overhead transparencies for the projector and casting the image onto the wall or ceiling near a particular activity requiring support. Like road signs, self-help visuals should be displayed according to need.

RESPONDING TO LEARNERS' NEEDS

As we plan our lesson content, we will need to consider the kinds of special language that learners might require in order to express themselves and function as a responsible partner or member of a group. The development of social skills required to design and agree questions in a group to draw up a survey, for example, needs to go hand in hand with the analysis of the language required to carry out the activity. If our aim is that our learners should increasingly employ the target language to carry out transactions, instructions and requests, the necessary language will need to be progressively built into our teaching programmes.

USE OF THE GRAFITTI BOARD, NOTEBOOK OR SCRIBBLE PAD

We can never hope to cover every need, but we can encourage learners to keep a note of where the target language ran out in the process of a task and where they needed to use English. This can be done by using the whiteboard as a grafitti board or a scribble pad. Otherwise, a straightforward notebook will suffice.

That's a good idea; *What did you say? Let X have a say*; *In my opinion*; *I agree*; *I disagree*; *You can't ask that!* Perhaps these are the kinds of things that the 14-year old learner wanted to say, as she referred to the posters of pencils and rulers on her own classroom wall, when she said *Yeah! But, I know those ones. I need new ones to say what I want to say!*. If our learners are to use language readily and more spontaneously, a gradual and systematic programme of learning must be developed, revisited and extended according to their growing needs.

5. Reaching for the sky: questions for self-evaluation and departmental development

Many issues have been raised in this Pathfinder and there will be many questions that we need to ask of our learners, our colleagues and ourselves. Some strategies suggested may be already familiar features of our practice, others may appeal but may be very different from our current teaching style. Some activities may seem to involve a high degree of risk and seem more controversial. Change comes slowly. We are all reluctant to an extent about stepping outside of the circle of existing experience. This is just as much the case for learners as for ourselves. There is much to be gained by involving learners, discussing ways in which to improve the quality of their learning environment and negotiating ways in which to promote more spontaneous use of the target language.

KEEPING ON TARGET

What am I aiming to change?	Next lesson	Next term	Next year
In myself			
With my colleagues			
With my learners			

Some strategies can be implemented swiftly with only a modicum of change. We can all review the range of resources and reference materials that we offer without too much threat. We can consider the use of accommodation and assess its suitability for more flexible whole class, individual, pair and group activities. We can have a look at our wall displays and explore possibilities of supporting older learners by the use of relevant displays of language which change according to the needs of the activity. Perhaps the idea of learners identifying their own language shortcomings by the use of a grafitti board seems exciting and feasible. Other strategies may require longer term planning to allow for the development of a culture where mutual respect and tolerance of error exist and communication in the target language is perceived as natural. The planner above invites readers to note down if they wish ideas they they would like to trial in the short and longer term. Planning involves ourselves, our learners and our colleagues. Keeping on target relies on co-operation, collaboration and consistency.

The real challenge of keeping on target is the development of independence in our learners . This is related closely to the development of communicative competence. The more successful and confident they feel the easier it will be to sustain motivation and use of the target language.

If we are feeling brave, we could ask ourselves the following questions in relation to the range and scope of our current teaching programme.

- Is there an abundance of content-based activities with defined outcomes which restrict learners to low level linguistic tasks?
- Do we strike a balance between activities which develop grammatical competence, socio-linguistic competence, discursive competence and strategic competence?
- Do learners explore and experiment with language and discover grammar for themselves or is the study of grammar always divorced from their direct experience?
- Do we build in opportunities for them to talk for different purposes and to different audiences, so that they increase their awareness of resister and idiom first hand?
- Do they move from simple to complex use of language?
- Do they have opportunities to hold conversations, sequence their ideas, give structured talks, stage an argument, persuade, discuss in pairs and in groups?
- How can we build in such opportunities regularly and support both the linguistic and the social skills necessary to fulfil the requirements of the activities effectively?
- Are we sure that we involve our learners sufficiently at all stages of the learning, drawing on their creativity and imagination in terms of linguistic problem solving not purely in terms of creative outcomes?
- How competent are they at using dictionaries, paraphrase, metaphor, gesture and intonation?
- Can they convey their message and more by the end of their period of language study?

The central message is that keeping on target is a much more complex business than it appears to be, if our sights are set on learners using the target language for the purposes of all classroom communication. We are at a very early stage at national level and will not be able to assess the long term effects of increased use of the target language for a few years yet. However, we are already recognising benefits in listening skills, pronunciation and intonation and in learners' willingness to sustain concentration and motivation, By gradually extending the range and quality of learning opportunities offered and sharing high expectations with our learners of what can be achieved. The sky is the limit.